TELLING THE
BEES

TELLING THE BEES

Poems by
Faith Shearin

Stephen F. Austin State University Press
Nacogdoches, Texas

For information address:
Stephen F. Austin State University Press
1936 North Street, LAN 203
Nacogdoches, TX 75962

sfapress@sfasu.edu

Design: Russell K. Allen
Author Photograph: Gordon Kreplin

LIBRARY OF CONGRESS CATALOGING-IN-PUBLICATION DATA

Shearin, Faith
Telling the Bees/Faith Shearin—1st ed.
p.cm,
ISBN 978-1-62288-091-1

I. Title

First Edition: 2015

Acknowledgments: The poems in this volume have appeared previously, sometimes in slightly different form, in the following journals and reviews:

Alaska Quarterly Review: "My Weight On Other Planets" and "Things We're All Too Young To Know"
Cincinnati Review: "Dogs Waiting for their Owners"
Cold Mountain Review: "Snow", "Wedding Dresses", "The Carnival", and "Crabs"
Comstock Review: "My Mother, Painting the Sea" and "Gravity"
Connotation Press: An Online Artifact: "So Many Things Can Ruin a Picnic" and "The Ones Who Stay"
North American Review: "Climbing the Lighthouse" and "Snowy Owl"
Parody: "A Few Things I Ate"
Poetry East: "Heart Island", "Rewind", "Blessing of the Animals", "Balloons", "Scurvy", "Gravity is Getting Stronger", "My Daughter Describes the Tarantula", "Suicides", "The Sound of a Train", "My Mother's Lost Keys", "My Father, Taking Pills", "Gretel's Bread Crumbs", and "My Mother, Pretending to Move to Alaska"
Southern Review: "Living Beside Water"
Spoon River Poetry Review: "Doom Town"
The Bark: "The Dog Brought Morning"
The Sun: "The Dog Watched Television"

Thanks to Tom and Mavis, my sister and brother, my parents and grandparents, and all the Friday Writers. Thanks to Garrison Keillor for the encouragement and the beautiful readings.

for the Friday Writers: Melanie Sumner, Adrienne Su, Raymond Atkins, and Diana Rico

and in memory of my grandfather, Henry Grayson Spruill, who was always glad to see me.

Table of Contents

I am out with lanterns, looking for myself.
                    --Emily Dickinson in a letter to EG Holland, 1885

You ask of my companions. Hills, sir, and the sundown, and a dog as large as myself, that my father bought me. They are better than beings because they know but do not tell...
                    --Emily Dickinson in a letter to TW Higginson, 1862

TELLING THE BEES

The Carnival

It will be spring when
the carnival comes to town.
Great tents will rise like bread
under the day's heat
and the ferris wheel will begin
its orbit. It is thrilling
how much can change
in a single night, how
an empty field can fill with color
and screams, with pale candy
spun from sugar and air.
Those cheap stuffed animals
were never meant to be won
and the fried dough
wasn't meant to be eaten.
If you walk through the fun house
there are mirrors that remember
who you were in a fairy tale:
a dwarf, a giant ruler
of beanstalks. As quickly
as it arrives it will vanish,
while you are humming
or sleeping, while you are lost
in thought. The grass in the field
will recall the shape of what
was pressed against it for a day,
or a week, then it will be as if
it never happened at all, as if
there are no fortune tellers,
no boxes of popcorn, no tickets
in your pocket, no buckets of rings
you toss into the dark.

Gravity Is Getting Stronger

You may have noticed how weak you feel
in the morning, how each of your feet
weighs as much as unhappiness. Maybe

your coffee cup is as heavy as a lie
or your morning paper is made of stone.
Once you are middle aged, gravity

increases. This is why you do not skip
or run squealing across the lawn
in the evening, your laughter weightless.

You are the opposite of the astronaut
who floats in a rocket with windows
made of perspective. You cannot admire

the delicate greens of earth, cannot
see the moon's white beach. Even the couch
your grandmother gave you is so full

of memory it cannot be lifted; even
the promises you made so easily
all those years ago have gained weight.

At first gravity was what kept you
from floating away. Now it is the thing
that reminds you of all the places

you will not go; it is as relentless
as the seasons, which will not stop
twirling, determined to make you dizzy.

The Old Mother

One day the Old Mother went to the pediatrician's office.
She had no baby in need of shots, no child
with an earache or sore throat. She sat a long time
in the waiting room and, when she was called,
told the doctor about the crying in the night,
the way her baby seemed to be made of shadows.
She visited the elementary school where, for years,
she waited in the grass with other parents
for the internal ringing of bells, the moment when
her own particular child would emerge from
a crowd. The Old Mother watched each
child leaving the stern brick building but none of them
had the face and scent that belonged to her.
She went to the zoo and watched the animals
by herself, unable to impart any particular knowledge.
She watched the giraffe with its endless neck
and disappointing head; she watched the prairie dogs
sticking their noses out of fake holes. The Old Mother
went to the ice cream shop where she used to ask
for cups instead of cones; she went to the playground
where she used to sit on a bench and watch
hours of climbing and swinging. She wandered
the neighborhood pushing her own confusion
in a stroller, her children lurking in the early
strands of evening, the softness of her abdomen,
the new complaints of her feet.

Living Beside Water

When you live beside water there are two
of everything: the house on land
and the house in the sea, deep green,

glassy, the porch disappearing
in the afternoon. There are the trees

that reach into the sky, thin and prim,
then the trees made of liquid darkness
which even boats can erase

with their going. When we float
in our canoe we travel beside

ourselves and can reach down
into the water to touch our own hands
which are clammy and flat; we press

our faces against the faces
we have lost. Our street of houses

glistens and expands: its light lit twice,
its details blurry as the evening
dissolves. There are the real objects:

piers, hammocks, laughter,
then the wet painting of those things.

When I leave my island I leave
behind the only reflection of myself
I have ever liked: the one that ruined

Narcissus, who spent years
pondering his beauty in the water.

Heart Island

Between New York and Canada are the Thousand Islands,
each one about the right size for a house with a yard,
each one owned by a person who imagined

a life surrounded by water. Among these, Heart Island
has a castle where no one lives. It was built by
George Boldt, owner of a fancy New York hotel,

for his pretty wife, Louise. This was the Gilded Age
and the great stone stairways were as grand
as love. But Louise did not live long and the castle

was never finished. She was never caressed
by the light in the windows, did not stand
in the highest tower admiring her view. Love is

like this: a castle built for someone who will not
enjoy it. So much time spent planning the light fixtures,
the color of the carpet, while love's object is elsewhere.

Maybe Louise wanted the castle and maybe she didn't.
Either way, it stands empty, gazing out at the water:
its windows without glass, its kitchen always cold, its rooms

so bare it's hard to believe pleasure ever designed them.

Things We're All Too Young To Know

We're all too young to know when we will die,
or what will cause it, too young to discover how little
our lives matter, how no amount of planning

or caution will save us. We are too young
to know this is the last vacation we will take
with our grandfather: this one by the shore

where the wind blows only from the east.
We're too young to have grown children
or arthritis or thin hair, too young to choose

a spouse or profession, to drive a car safely
through the narrow streets of winter.
We're always too young to have someone

we love tell us they are leaving. We're too young
for root canals and retirement, too young
for sex, or even the pictures that suggest

its intimate details. We're too young to play
with matches or to understand why chocolate
is usually eaten after dinner. We're certainly

too young to know who we will be when
we grow up, to know that the sky's blues
and grays are indifferent to our luck.

We're too young for taxes or childbirth,
for dead pets, or the day when we no longer
have parents. We're too young to find

our own faces foreign: the happiness and sorrow
visible, our skin folded like paper. And we're
definitely too young for high heels and lipstick,
too young to sit at a bar with a glass of something hard.

Scurvy

When sailors crossed the oceans
their gums bled and their teeth
grew as loose as screen doors

in the wind. They ate old biscuits
and salted meats and bruises
appeared like stains over

their bodies and then they began
unhealing: the arm they broke
as a child when they fell from

a tree unmended and the gash
in their knee when they were thrown
from a horse reopened. All the old

wounds were new, as if
time had undone itself, as if
each injury is permanent,

just waiting to show itself again.
It was worse the second time,
not having fallen from a tree

or horse, but suffering anyway,
in the middle of the ocean, where,
for weeks, no land was visible.

My Mother, Painting the Sea

She is sunburned in a folding chair and, before her,
an easel, and, beyond that, the eager flapping of the sea;
she has been painting all afternoon while I have floated
among the pages of magazines, wearing a wet bathing suit
and eating a sandwich. Her hand seems to be made
of color and the scene in her brush is already disappearing,
the day tired. She has remade the waves
in a flat world, without sound. On her canvas, it will not
grow dark and we will not pack our bags and walk
through the dunes to the empty cups in our cottage.
Painting, she is quiet, unworried, determined
to make a life out of light and shadow.

So Many Things Can Ruin a Picnic

So many things can ruin a picnic --
mosquitoes, for instance, arriving
in a gray hum or black flies or a wind
strong enough to blow napkins
over the lawn like white butterflies,
steaks stolen by dogs, unruly fire,
thunderstorms that come on suddenly,
clouds converging over a field,
where you have just unpacked
your basket. It's amazing, really,
that people have picnics at all
considering how many plates
have fallen in the dirt and how many
hot dogs have erupted in black blisters,
how many children have climbed hills
alive with poison ivy and how much ice
has melted before the drinks
were ever poured. It's amazing
how many people still want to eat
on a blanket anyway, are still willing
to take their chances, to endure
whatever may fall or bite. Either they
don't consider the odds of success
or they don't care. Some of them
must not mind the stains on their pants,
the heavy watermelon that isn't sweet
once it's carved. Some must understand
the way lightning is likely to strike
an open field. Even so -- they wrap up
a few pieces of fried chicken, fold
a tablecloth until it is as small as hope.
They carry an umbrella or a jacket
that they accidentally drop on the ground
where it fills with bees. They leave
the houses they built to keep them safe
and eat uncovered, ignoring the thunder,
their egg salad growing dangerously hot.

Hating School

It began sometime after first grade and became
an annual affliction; the store windows filled
with notebooks and lunch boxes and my daughter
was seized by dread. All summer she was happy
in her bathing suit, floating in the pool's chemical blue.
She slept as much as she liked and ate ice cream
and lived in the towns she built out of sticks
and silence. She sat a long time on our front porch
sketching her dogs, in profile, and ate her supper
thoughtfully, a book opened beside her plate.
Then the air grew cooler and a certain sorrow
settled over her face. The other children liked
Halloween and the rushing waterfall
of hallways and the chance to see their friends.
But my daughter dreaded all of it: the bells,
the tests, the afternoons when she stood alone
on the playground, watching. The trees
began removing their bright costumes
and my daughter stood in that narrowing
light and unhappiness became a staircase
she climbed each morning; it was a room full
of desks, the weight of knowing she was different.

Secrets

They go to the dark, unloved places: into buildings
where no one lives, where windows have broken
and walls have fallen and all the furniture
is full of birds. Secrets are at the bottom

of each tea cup, at the bottom of the ocean
where fish swim through their ruined remains.
Secrets are in hospitals where doctors
hide them in the sleeves of their white coats,

write them sometimes in files that will be forgotten.
There are secrets in desks and curtains, secrets
in trees and secrets in the uncombed hair
of young girls. There are secrets in blood

which even microscopes cannot find, secrets
in the dens of foxes and the seeds
of apples. There are secrets on abandoned
playgrounds where the swings move

back and forth without children or wind.
Some secrets are alive and they flutter in closets,
nibble television cords, steal crumbs. But others
are buried deeply in cemeteries

and safe deposit boxes and require no air.
Wine turns red with secrets; dresses carry them
in their skirts. I have seen a secret coiled
like a snake at the center of a dinner party;

I have walked through parks where they fell
around me like leaves. I have kept them,
which is not as easy as it sounds: some howl
at night, transformed by the presence of the moon.

Some breathe fire and place the village in danger.
Some get caught in my throat like a bone,
and I must pretend I am not choking...

Lancelot

Lancelot was raised by the Lady of the Lake
on her island, in her palace,
which changed color like the trees.
He knew the tides that rose and fell
like a kingdom, the way fish would swim
in that deeper, quieter place, their scales
like armor. He knew about lures
and lines and patience, about the places
where light is ghostly and unknown.
His guardian was green-eyed
and gauzy and there were things
she did not tell him; he floated
sometimes in her boats which were
as white and elegant as swans.
An island is a circle and to be raised
on one is to know how stories end.
Lancelot did not know where
he came from, did not know yet
that his real mother was
The Queen of Great Griefs,
did not sense his own destiny
at the round table, behind that curtain
of mists. But he must have noticed
how the waves ate his coastline,
how any long walk returned him
to his beginning. The Lady of the Lake
told Lancelot that, as a knight,
he would need two hearts:
one soft and one hard. No wonder
he sharpened his knives and practiced
gathering oysters and crabs. No wonder
he stood over the lake in winter,
transfixed by the way water became glass.

My Driveway

It curves dangerously up the side of a mountain,
swerves violently before settling
into a long incline beside a cliff. Early on
my father decided to park at the bottom
and climb on foot through the dust
of summer. I often saw his dog first,
her leash floating behind her like a scarf.
Then there was my friend Anna
whose van sent up one plume of smoke,
then another, her children emerging
as if from a dream. My visitors got stuck
in the curve itself which demanded speed
and belief; it asked drivers to turn hard
before they could see where
they were going. Several workmen
my husband hired would not attempt
the driveway, even our moving van hesitated
at the bottom, our furniture and dishes
sliding back. I was afraid to drive it,
then I longed for it: the rush up,
the sharp turn, the sight of the cabin
waiting in its meadow of disbelief.
Deer stepped into the driveway and
wild dogs and turkeys walking slowly
into morning. Clouds drifted up my driveway
and wrapped our windows in forgetfulness.
I was connected to the world below
by uncertainty and pebbles
which glowed the way Gretel's pebbles
glowed when she remembered home.

My Mother's Lost Keys

There must be a place in a forest where they hang
from the trees or a deep sewer where they glitter
beneath the swimming rats. Maybe there is
a diner where they are placed on the tables
like silverware or a child's closet where
they are kept in a box like race cars or marbles.
My mother lost so many keys during
my childhood, slipped them into her purse
or pocket where they vanished the way
years vanish, the way sanity vanishes
if you are angry. We had new ones made
but the originals must be somewhere:
in abandoned buckets of beach sand,
in a freezer like ice cubes, in the night sky like
so many dead stars. I think they would help me
unlock certain doors; I believe
they wait for me like birthday candles.

My Weight on Other Planets

My daughter told me I would weigh 25 pounds on the moon:
my boots pale, my hair made of wind. On Venus or Uranus
I would be my ideal weight: 120 pounds,
my mouth as soft as clouds. On Pluto I would weigh
as much as our tiny dog, who could fit easily
in anyone's pocket, her nose cold. It was Jupiter
I should avoid, she said, for here I would become
so heavy I might be related to elephants
or death. I suppose I knew this already?
On earth I weigh more during an argument
but less when I am swimming, more
when I am disliked, less when I have been
singing in the trees. Once, in a field with a friend,
I was weightless: my breath invisible,
my thoughts like angels or kites.

Candling

This is how my grandmothers looked into
the eggs without disturbing them:
the room was darkened and they shined
a light through the mystery of the shell.
After a week in the incubator's heat
a web of fine blood vessels appeared,
sometimes the knot of an eye.
They showed me how certain chicks
started then stopped: a blood ring
around the absence, a ghostly shape
inside without wings or feet.
Sometimes they candled the suspicious
eggs a second time and a third,
measured the air space, watched
as dark and light arranged themselves
inside those miniature worlds.

Lizzie Borden

She had a wandering alibi: first she was in the back yard,
then in the loft, then in the barn, eating pears. She claimed
she was wearing a heavy bengaline dress
in the late August heat of the murders. This was months
after her father beheaded all her pigeons

with an axe. I suppose there were a few unexplained
robberies in the neighborhood; it is also true
that Lizzie stood to inherit a fortune. One neighbor
saw her burning a stained apron after the deaths;
one official noticed her graduation ring on her father's

lifeless hand. She became an opera, a play.
No one can really know the darkness inside a family.
I think of the things she must have felt,
the arguments her neighbors did not overhear.
I think of her pigeons: unable to move or coo

or deliver their delicate messages. And Lizzie:
in the back yard, in the loft, in the barn, eating pears.

Crabs

My parents moved to a cottage by the sea
and my grandmother arrived with her twenty suitcases
and hand lotions and we spent a week together,
sunning ourselves. We wore matching
bathing suits and sunburns and we built
castles too close to the tide: empires with tiny lives.
Then she decided we should cook crabs.
We stepped into the seafood shop, a cold box
of odor, and looked at the creatures pulled
from the salt of their dreams. They were frozen:
washed ashore on a beach of ice, and death
was a place you could see in their eyes.
There were eels that reminded me
of depths and currents and oysters as soft
as tongues in the bumpy mouths of their shells.
We bought a box of crabs and these were
fiercely alive: their eyes drops of color, their claws
opening and closing on misfortune. We prepared
to steam them and I hid my face in a pillow
while my grandmother dropped each one
into a shallow pan. We were sitting together
on the sofa when we saw them erupt
like lava: overflow onto the counter and floor.
They moved sideways in their bright armor
and they were everywhere
and we were afraid. We hopped on the furniture,
the floor dangerous, and we did not eat them,
even when my father came home and
collected them easily and returned them
to the unhappiness of their box. We took those
crabs back to the shore where they went on
following the tides, and rearranging the sand,
and holding their claws high like torches.

My Father, Taking Pills

It is morning and he has not eaten though he has
managed a half dozen cups of tea with honey
in his plaid nightshirt, the dog at his feet.
He keeps the bottles near his bed
and they are brown with plastic caps
and he shakes the pills into his palm
where they glisten for a minute:
one red and blue, another amber,
several hard and white like stones.
Then, one by one, he swallows them
with his head tilted back and his eyes closed.
He sits very still when he is finished.
I remember him young in his business suit
with his black hair and his fast walk;
I remember when he left the kitchen
with nothing but coffee. The pills
fall on the floor sometimes where they are
crushed by furniture or feet; the bottles
have his name on their labels and expiration dates
and warnings and they watch him eat his breakfast.
They glow when the sun is inside them.

Predators

Before zoos and pruned neighborhoods, before
man chopped down forests and shot beasts,
there were predators in the darkness.
Once, there were leviathans and cave lions
and great lumbering, hungry bears.
They didn't live in cages or on tiny slivers
of wilderness, nearly extinct. They decorated
our cave paintings and kept us awake
beside our islands of fire. We were different
when we knew we could be eaten: more humble,
more alert. We feared the man-eaters
but we also conjured their spirits,
dressed in their skins. Now we have beaten
them back, we are weaker, more defenseless.
It is the remains of our own objects
that watch us from the woods instead:
legless mattresses, shattered televisions
with antennae like antlers, displaced toilets
white with embarrassment along the banks
of our rivers, a refrigerator that could lure
a child into its airless emptiness: hungry and hot.

Telling the Bees

In Europe's towns, two hundred years ago, bees
were believed to be little emissaries to God.
They were loved for the way they made food
that tasted like the village itself: its flowers
and fields and rains and grief. You told the bees
when someone inside your house took ill;
it was the bees you consulted
when you found yourself pregnant. You served
the bees cake before a party and consoled them
when your father died. You spoke to the hive,
which is mostly feminine: that fat queen
and her ladies in waiting, eternally listening
in a castle made of wax. And the bees turned
the news, all news, to honey --
dark or golden, enough for everyone to survive
winter, enough to sweeten dreams or tea.

Natural Disasters

During natural disasters two enemy animals
will call a truce, so during a hurricane
an owl will share a tree with a mouse
and, during an earthquake, you might find
a mongoose wilted and shivering
beside a snake. The bear will sit down
in a river and ignore the passing salmon
just as the lion will allow the zebra
to walk home without comment.
I love that there are exceptions.
At funerals and weddings, for example,
the aunts who never speak nod
politely to one another. When my mother
was sick even the prickly neighbors
left flowers and cakes at our door.

Coffins

People were afraid of being buried alive
so they asked that axes and shovels
and trumpets be placed beside them.
They wanted coffins with windows

and air holes, lids that would spring open
if their bodies shifted in the depths
of that eternal rest. One model had
a tube to the ground's surface;

another sported flags and bells
and music. Any movement of the chest
would cause a commotion --
A few came with a telephone

so the deceased could call relatives
and tell them it was a mistake,
they weren't dead after all, and
just like that, they would rejoin

the living, stepping gingerly out
of their hole. The coffin would open
and the lights would blaze and there,
in the silent graveyard: life.

The nearly dead would return
to all of it: spring cleaning, taxes,
and death would become something
that almost happened but didn't,

like one car skidding towards another
but turning away, like a storm
that struck some other town,
like a season that never arrived:

leaves and snow unfallen,
night never short, never long.

Snowy Owl

The winter my father nearly died snowy owls
became confused and left the arctic

for places to the south; one stood
behind his bedroom with yellow eyes

and a black beak and a body made of cream.
This was the year the owls mistook airports for

grasslands and many were killed
trying to land, the year they were found

as far away as Florida, haunting
beaches and marshes, their bodies

the size of canopic jars, their heads turning
and turning until too many things were visible.

My father was watched by one owl,
a male, who stood alone in the southern

darkness, speaking to him
of melting ice, of change.

My Grandparents' Generation

They are taking so many things with them:
their sewing machines and fine china,

their ability to fold a newspaper
with one hand and swat a fly.

They are taking their rotary telephones,
and fat televisions, and knitting needles,

their cast iron frying pans, and Tupperware.
They are packing away the picnics

and perambulators, the wagons
and church socials. They are wrapped in

lipstick and big band music, dressed
in recipes. Buried with them: bathtubs

with feet, front porches, dogs without leashes.
These are the people who raised me

and now I am left behind in
a world without paper letters,

a place where the phone
has grown as eager as a weed.

I am going to miss their attics,
their ordinary coffee, their chicken

fried in lard. I would give anything
to be ten again, up late with them

in that cottage by the river, buying
Marvin Gardens and passing go,

collecting two hundred dollars.

The Wife

She has worn so many veils that I cannot find her face.
I watched my grandmothers practice her ancient manners;
they were bent over her housework,
served men first, starched shirts and shone shoes.
The wife began as property and she came with
little gifts: a frying pan, a cow, a lace nightgown;
she pretends not to remember this. Husbands
and in-laws like her to be tidy and quiet, to make
a little money but not too much. Children hope
she is selfless and kind. Can the wife reinvent herself
or is she forever a maker of lunches and cleaner
of toilets? Is her name eternally less important?
I watched her for years, trying to decide if I could
fit myself into her narrow description. I want marriage
to be about love but it is also about history.
The wife is a ghostly white shape, a hand,
a thing given away. What does a bride wish
when she stands in plastic on a cliff made of cake?
What does she feel when she walks in a white rice rain?

Doom Town

We were invented to practice destruction:
a family of mannequins, our clothes
chosen by scientists.

The food in our pantry was never
meant to be eaten;
our homes were thin and sudden,

our warehouses false, our train tracks
unable to produce a train. We stayed
where we were placed, doing the things

that suggested who we were:
setting the table for a meal
we could not imagine, mowing

the grassless desert sand.
We should not have been surprised
when the sky turned red;

we should not have been sad
since our life before had never
been our own. When the day

broke open, our windows melted
and we fell over and came apart.
Our life was so brief, so planned.

Gretel's Bread Crumbs

There was no time to collect stones for that second trip
into the forest so Gretel stayed hungry, her bread
in her pocket. When she dropped each crumb
she was forgetting the way home. First she forgot
the blue front door, then her own narrow bed, then the place
by the window where she watched the stars grow cold.
She forgot her mother, already dead, and supper,
and the afternoon when her father taught her
to tie her shoes. She was forgetting home: the forest
tall, then taller, its shadows deep and complex.

The Bees Dance

They have one dance
that means the nectar
is far away and another
that shows the sweetness
is nearby. The bees speak
of the position of the sun,
of distances, of how deep
and meaningful certain
trees may be. The tremble dance,
one of my favorites, means there
is no need to go on gathering.
In the spring, when the hive
is wondrous with honey,
ten thousand bees will leave
with the old queen to start over
and a few hundred will hunt
for a new home and their dances
are about how grand
or lackluster their new finds
might be. The bees dance
maps and enthusiasm;
they dance light and fields;
the bees waggle;
the bees dance.

Post Office

If you ask, I will tell you
how my uncle pushed me on a cart
and my grandfather's dog waited
outside in a patch of sleep. I will tell you
how my grandmother stood
at the counter in a navy blue suit,
her mouth traced in scarlet,
and how the packages smelled
like distant towns and the PO boxes
with golden doors waited
to be opened. The floors were
polished green and the break room
had a clock with a stern face
and a cooler of cokes in sexy bottles;
a cold fog rose around them
and to touch them was to
touch winter. I loved the books
of stamps and the rolls of tape
and the way messages were arriving
and departing in bundles. I was
too short to be seen by the customers
unless my grandfather held me
over the counter. This was a town
of disappearing farms and increasing
cemeteries. By the time I was tall
the downtown would be a memory of
brick buildings filling with wind and mice.
But this was before all that, when
my relatives woke in the dark,
their dreams full of delivery.
Sometimes my uncle let me sit
in his car before he drove away,
down the unpaved past, his back seat
white with envelopes.

Floods and Fires

When I was nine our house burned down;
we stood on the lawn in pajamas

and watched our rooms flicker;
it was winter and the streets smelled

of sleep and snow. After hurricanes
my father, in a canoe, paddled through

our sunken city: he found the roof
of our garage, our mailbox filling itself

with fish. Once, his van rolled backwards
and vanished in a river while he stood

nearby. Some people polish
their belongings, hand them down

from one generation to another,
but ours are incinerated or they drift

to the ocean floor where they join
the shipwrecks, the cargo that will never

arrive at its intended destination,
the bones, the whales that once had legs,

long ago, before they stopped walking
the earth, before they learned to sing.

Brontosaurus

He was created during my childhood by attaching
the head of one dinosaur to the body of another.
He was given a name and habits:
a diet, a landscape, an approximate size
for his children. I went with my class
more than once to admire
his oversized jaws and delicate backbone.
This was back when Russia was the Soviet Union,
when Pluto was a planet, and ulcers
were caused by stress. I believed in this
fictitious dinosaur the same way I believed
in all the others, liked him more maybe,
though I was never exactly sure why.

Suicides

There was the one who walked into a river
with her pockets full of stones and the one
who started her car with the garage door closed,
determined to drive herself elsewhere.
The youngest went into the kitchen
and placed her head where she had
so often placed chickens or hams.
These were the women whose voices
I carried in my backpacks, whose books
moved with me from one city to another
and, one day, I realized I had outlived
all of them. I was sad that they could
not describe the other world,
that they offered no map to old age.
Was it dangerous to write? I began
to walk more carefully beside rivers,
to eat cold food, to let someone else
back the car out of the driveway.

A Few Things I Ate

There are a few things I'm sorry I ate: a piece of fried chicken
in an all night diner that bled when I cut into it,
a soup in an elegant French restaurant where I encountered
a mysterious ring of plastic. Also: a bowl of spaghetti served
with so many long strands of hair I wondered who,
in the kitchen, had gone bald. I'm sorry I ate the fast food
cookies that tasted like paper the same way I am sorry
I let certain men kiss me or hold my hand. I'm especially sorry
I ate a certain hot dog on a train that had been twirling for days
on a luke warm display. Forgive me for all that cafeteria food
in college: packaged, bland, frozen so long it could not
remember flavor. And, hungry in my dorm, I ate bags
of stale lies from vending machines, once even a pair
of expired Twinkies filled with a terrible chemical cream
I am still digesting. After my daughter was born I bought
so much organic baby food my husband found the jars
everywhere: little glass wishes. One winter I ate exotic fruits
from upscale stores so expensive I might have flown instead
to a distant tropical island. Then, careless, I ate
from containers only my microwave understood. I know
what food is supposed to be but often isn't; I know
who I might have been if I ate whatever I should have eaten.
Remember the time we ate Ethiopian food and spent
a week dreaming so vividly our real life grew pale?
Or the day we ate so much spice in our Thai food
that our mouths were softer? I'm not sorry I ate
all those ice cream sandwiches from my grandmother's
freezer and drank those Pepsis with her on the way
to Kmart to buy more pink, plastic toys. She liked
the way sugar made me lively and, anyway,
she was suggesting the possibility of pleasure.
She made a vegetable soup that simmered all day
on the stove: growing deeper, more convincing,
and a carrot cake with cream cheese icing that floated
on my tongue like love. Now I am middle aged I am fat
and eating salads or, before bed, talking myself

into rice cakes that taste like despair. My father
is diabetic and must have everything whole wheat
and lean and my sister can't have any salt. I'm sorry
I ate all that cereal when we first got married,
by myself in the kitchen, the milk pale and worried.
Remember how I covered my fruit with cheese
and mayonnaise? I'm not sorry, whatever
you might say. Then there were the lunches
we ate on the beach, watching the seals
sun themselves: thick chicken sandwiches wrapped
in a foil so silver they must have been valuable.

Retired

On the island where I was a child
nearly everyone was retired, their fortunes

already made. Death was around them
the way water was around our streets.

They taught me how to go fishing
without catching fish; the tide's breath

was marked in notebooks they kept
beneath their pillows. One old lady

fed me chocolates from a tin
until my teeth were stained by greed.

The old do things slowly so I grew used
to grocery store lines

that did not move, cars that stopped
in the middle of the road. One man spent

a whole day helping me bury a squirrel;
we wrote odes and dirges

to the way it once hurried and planned.

There Were Giants in Those Days

There were giants in those days; I don't know
where they have gone. We've found their tools
though we can't lift them, have seen
what they built on Easter island, their heads
wrapped in clouds. What did they eat?
Some were twenty feet tall and they had
a view. I'm talking about six-fingered hands,
thigh bones as long as winter nights,
feet that could crush history. Some of us
must be related to the skeletons found
in Wisconsin or France; sometimes,
in a circus, we meet a man who cannot stop
growing and, when we shake his hand,
we remember. There were giants in those days
and they knew what skyscrapers
and mountains know; they could not sit
in our chairs, would not be able to stand up
in our rooms. Their hats were the size
of planets; they did not know the word vast.
My desire to find them is cast in amber.
I don't know where they have gone.

Wedding Dresses

Packed away in attics, wrapped in plastic,
pressed into boxes as big as coffins
were the wedding dresses of my aunts
and grandmothers. They rustled

the way snakes rustle in a pile of leaves.
Were they dangerous or angry? A single
day in the world had not been enough.
I found them with my cousins,

during games of hide and seek,
or while dressing up in other clothes:
floppy hats, shoes so tall we could not
keep our balance. They had a stillness

around them that reminded me of graveyards:
their lace no longer white, as if time
had steeped it in tea. They were fitted
and stern or as showy as blossoms

in spring: big skirts, trains that followed
a bride like a history. Sometimes
my grandmother took one out
to show us and, flung across the bed,
I could see the shape of the woman

who wore it, long ago, marching
into the unknown. Sometimes
we found a veil, wrapped separately,
and it dangled like a jellyfish

in our hands. The dresses were
as empty as seashells; like unicorns
they favored the attention of young girls.
They were impractical: not made for dancing

or reaching, meant to be worn once
then never again. They seemed both
ignorant and wise: snowy owls
perched in a closet made of night.

Clue

We bought the board game, Clue, at the start of summer
and carried it with us wherever we went: to my mother's hysterectomy, to
the week at the beach when your father's breathing
became a dragon. We took it to a mountain cabin
and placed it on a table in a main room so it was the game
we played with my grandparents, with visiting children,
with strangers in airports and cousins in hotel rooms.
We were trying to discover who committed the fictional
murder in what room with what object. There was a ballroom
where we did not go dancing, a billiard room where
we did not play pool, a secret passage we took many times
to the silky silence of the conservatory. My daughter asked
how you kill someone with a candlestick; I said you could
set them on fire in their bedroom at night; you said
you could hit them very hard on the head. There had been
too many intrusions, too many sicknesses. Maybe
Mr. Green did it in the kitchen with a wrench or maybe
Mrs. White did it in the library with a lead pipe.
Our daughter was good at the game; she understood
there were cards you did not have to show, questions
she could ask which would mislead other players.
Maybe I did it: I could not train the dog,
or apologize, or file books on a shelf according to subject.
My grandmother felt that Miss Scarlet could not have done it
because pretty women do not commit crimes. She was wrong,
of course, but I envied her conviction. We didn't know how
or when our parents got sick; we didn't know who
we were now. Once there was no murderer at all:
just two weapons and a room. Once a child guessed
the answer before the game had even begun, said:
Professor Plum, in the hall, with a rope, and it was true.

My Daughter Describes the Tarantula

Her voice is as lovely and delicate as a web.
She describes how fragile they are,
how they can die from a simple fall.
Then she tells me about their burrows
which are tidy and dry and decorated
with silk. They are solitary, she tells me,
and utterly mild, and when they are
threatened they fling their hairs, trying
not to bite. She says they are most
vulnerable when they molt: unable
to eat for days while they change.
They are misunderstood, she explains,
and suddenly her description becomes
personal. She wants to keep one
as a pet, to appreciate it properly,
to build it a place where it belongs.

Hormones

My hormones told me things; they spoke to me like Eve's snake,
like the mirror Snow White's stepmother hung in her heart,
like a vulture, circling. They made so many beasts appear
handsome, caused the acne and blushing, the desire,
the blood, the milk, the childbirth, and the time afterwards
when I was afraid. They controlled my hunger,
made my breasts ache. They brought the flashes
of heat and cold, the anger, the tears. They were inside me
but I could not see them; they pulled the strings
and I was a puppet, gesturing to the crowd. They were
the Pied Piper and I was the rats or the children, lured
from my familiar darkness by a music I could not understand.

Argos

He waited twenty years, which is more
than a hundred years for a dog, waited

the way dogs wait for their owners:
on porches and in fields, under trees

and at windows. His ears were alert,
even when he slept, and his eyesight

grew vague, watching for Odysseus
to emerge from the fabric

of the sea. He waited in the darkness,
after Penelope was asleep, the shroud

she was weaving and unweaving
silky in the moonlight. He watched

while suitors wrecked the hall, followed
Telemachus until he was no longer

a child. He grew old waiting, which is
what happens to dogs who love.

Lost Cities

It's the mythic cities I love, the ones no one
can be sure of. Give me Atlantis
with its wet beds and staircases,

its clocks stopped by tides.
Give me Camelot before
Guinevere and Lancelot undressed

their betrayal: the knights valiant
at their round table, Merlin wise

and reliable. Let El Dorado glitter
for everyone who went looking:
that city just out of reach, its palaces

and wine glasses and bathtubs
made of gold. May Colonel Fawcett

always search for the place he called Z:
his body immune to tropical diseases,
his desire like a rain forest.

Give me the lost cities: the ones
that may or may not exist; draw me

a map to whatever cannot be inhabited
or found. Take me yourself: by camel
or submarine or pack mule; show me how

it shimmers, how splendor fills the windows,
how the place we cannot locate

is the way we keep ourselves alive.

Asking the Boys To Dance

I didn't know yet that I shouldn't so, at my sixth grade dance,
I asked the boys to dance instead of waiting for them
to ask me. I walked over to the wall where they reclined
in poses meant to seem casual and asked the ones
I liked best, one after another, enjoying myself. I didn't
notice that the other girls weren't doing it. I knew, I guess,
that they were huddled together in perfumed clumps
that sounded like whispers and looked like feathered hair.
I don't remember whether or not I was pretty or whether
the boys seemed to like me, but I was not too worried
about their opinions. I wanted to dance and I knew
who I wanted to dance with and I walked across the empty
gymnasium that separated the sexes. Later, when I told
my Mother what I'd done, she was worried for me.
She explained the role of the woman: passive as an egg,
able to accept or decline. I don't remember liking dances
after that; I wanted to choose, not to be chosen.

Strangers

The dog barks at us sometimes, if she cannot
see us properly. She points her thin head
and makes her most vicious sounds
and, for a moment, we are strangers:
thieves, thugs, muggers. We are not
ourselves until her nose finds us beneath
our coats and perfume; we are not ourselves
until she licks away our disguises.

The Dog Brought Morning

The dog brought morning on her short legs,
her nose as cold as dew. It is difficult

to bring the day into each bed,
one after another, with a tongue
as gentle as light. Who knew that morning

could burrow under blankets? Who knew
it was so hungry or soft or eager?
Morning is about turning towards

something; it is a dog with fur
as strong as coffee, her paws
stepping out of night's river.

Hurricanes

We had parties to celebrate them on my childhood island:
violent storms that formed over a warm sea. Hurricanes had eyes
that were calm though, like cats, they chased their own tails.
We nailed Xs over our windows, bought gallon jugs

of water, moved the canoe to the living room. Feeling the wind
rise was like skipping school on a day when every class
had a test; it was the discovery that my heart was also
a kite. They were dangerous, I know,

but mostly we did not leave. We waited for the lights to fail,
the radio to grow weak. We liked the way our streets
became rivers, the way our cars sank and our garages
disappeared. We didn't want to live inland where the weather

was predictable and tame; we wanted to live on a thin, exposed
strip of sand where the ocean breathed like a dragon.
We liked tropical storms and nor'easters and old shipwrecks
which appeared like wooden bodies on the beach.

We liked the way the dunes were always moving,
blown into unexpected arrangements. Our friends
came over and we watched the water rise until everything floated.

Early Hominids

In one museum scene they are bent over fire
and in another they hold their first stone tools
while the ice age approaches. They have been
painting mastodons and mammoths
in their caves, art already in their animal grasp,
and they have been leaving footprints
in volcanic ash, shedding their skeletons
in deserts. They have begun the journey
from trees to suburbs, have been dressing
themselves in early hats and considering
an alphabet. The young neanderthal looks like
a boy who bit you on the playground
and the woman beside him might be the woman
we avoid at the grocery store. This is evolution:
hair loss, math, a desire for furniture. Already
they worry about predators and weather; already
they have designs for a more comfortable bed.

Servants

In college I read about Virginia Woolf and Edith Wharton
and I thought of their great minds and their long dresses
and their gilded friendships which involved tea

in the library or on the lawn. I thought of the places
they traveled and the weight of their trunks
and all the ways their marriages did or did not

please them. I thought of the dogs that followed
at their heels and the rooms and gardens they
decorated and the beaches where they

carried umbrellas. But I never once thought of
their servants. I didn't think of the cook who
woke up to make the fires of morning or the maids

who stood over a pot of hot soap, stirring the day.
I did not think of how someone dressed them
and scrubbed their floors, how someone

brought their dinner on a tray. It was years before
I knew they had them at all: invisible, unremembered,
people who gave their lives to drudgery. Now I

can barely write or finish a book for all the housework
and errands, now I think of them: knocking dust
from the curtains, carrying the rugs outside

each spring so they could beat them with a broom.

Blessing of the Animals

At my daughter's Catholic school there is
a blessing of the animals at which
the children line up with their fat hamsters
and gauzy goldfish, their dogs so old

they can barely climb the hill. They bring
their cats with bald patches
and their lizards sleeping in cages
under a fake sun. In the line
to the priest there are snakes

with white eyes and birds without songs.
There are ant farms and worms and rats
with long, exposed tails. The children
wait hours for their animals
to be blessed: for the priest's hand

to hover over the weight they carry.
They bring shoe boxes full of turtles,
hairy spiders, frogs with dry skin.
I like watching my daughter

among the other children: her dog
small in her arms, her gaze protective.
Children believe in the power
of animals, tucked into their feathers
and shells; they believe

in blessings: the sprinkle
of holy water, each tiny
unexplained life.

Disappearing Fathers

Sometime after I turned forty the fathers from my childhood
began disappearing; they had heart attacks
during business dinners or while digging their shovels
into a late April snow. Some fathers began forgetting things:
their phone numbers, which neighborhoods belonged
to them, which houses. They had a shortness of breath,
the world's air suddenly too thin, as if it came
from some other altitude. They were gone:
the fathers I had seen dissecting cars
in garages, the fathers with suits
and briefcases, the fathers who slipped down
rivers on fishing boats and the ones
who drank television and beer. Most of my friends
still had mothers but the fathers
were endangered, then extinct.
I was surprised, though I had always known
the ladies lasted longer; the fathers fooled me
with their toughness; I had been duped
by their jogging and heavy lifting, misled
by their strength when they slapped
me on the back or shook my hand. I kept imagining
I would see them again: out walking their dogs
on the roads near my childhood house,
lighting cigars on their porches, waving to me
from their canoes while I waited on shore.

The Ones Who Stay

There are the ones who leave and the ones who stay,
the ones who go to war and the ones
who wander the silent streets, waiting

for news. There are the ones who join the circus
or go on safari: the explorers, the astronauts,
then there are the people who never leave

their first neighborhood, their first house.
Odysseus spent years trying to come home
but Penelope never left. He was seduced

by women with islands and sung to by sirens;
he held the wind in a bottle. But Penelope
slept differently in the same bed, weaving

and unweaving the daily details while men
she did not love gathered in her kitchen.
Her face grew thinner, her son grew taller.

Is that a journey? The ones who leave
come back with stories: an excitement
in their eyes. But the ones who stay

witness little changes: dust, weather, breath.
What happens to them goes so slowly
it seems not to be happening at all.

Bicycles

The early ones had that oversized wheel at the front, handles
like antennae, a tiny wheel behind. If women could find their balance
they could ride them: the world suddenly more open,
encouraging. Dresses were shed or worn with bloomers
and the streets filled with spinning and baskets and little horns.
Maybe women could not vote; maybe the majority of professions
did not want them. But the bicycles were shiny and bright
and to ride one you pushed off into the soft air which
did not disapprove. Women left the house for awhile,
left the tending and ironing, the million rules about what
was lady-like and right. They leaned forward, pressed
hard on the pedals, watched the familiar landscape blur.

A Strange Rain

I felt differently about the world when I learned
it could rain animals. Frogs have fallen
on picnics and city streets, their wet bodies

as unexpected as forgiveness. No one knows
for sure how it happens: tornadoes,
invisible winds? But the most unexpected

things have dropped from a clear
and ordinary afternoon: jellyfish in England,
spiders in Argentina, worms in Louisiana.

Even money has fallen: 16th century coins
in the streets of modern Russia,
2000 Marks rained down on a pair

of Clergymen in Germany. Several poor
British school children found themselves
in a flurry of cash, their hands

filled with enough to buy chocolates.
Even the sky has secrets though
it hangs above us like something obvious

and knowable; even the sky is surprising.
It is not just the wallpaper for the sun
or moon, not just the darkness behind the stars.

My Mother, Pretending to Move to Alaska

For thirty years my mother pretended she was moving
to Alaska. She owned no maps of the state
and did not try to visit; she lived on a hot island
in North Carolina and could not drive
in the snow, owned a thin winter coat,
no boots or gloves. My mother survived things
she hated by pretending she was leaving:
baby showers, years of teaching in classrooms
where children built fleets of paper airplanes.
She told me sometimes about Alaska:
a place where she would live so far from
the neighbors they could not maintain an interest
in her business, a place where there
was so much snow she would not ever
mow the lawn. On bad days my mother imagined
who she would be in that eternal winter:
rugged, adventurous, warm because
she was not thin. My mother was going
to Alaska and if she never got there
it was because her Alaska was not on any map
and could not be reached by boat or bobsled;
her Alaska was a blizzard of privacy
and imagination, its borders hidden or revealed
by the snow drifts in her mind.

Disappearances

There are so many ways for a woman to disappear.
She may vanish beneath a veil or behind
a stack of dishes. She might take a man's name

and forget her own. She may wait outside
her child's music lesson until she is a chair
or a magazine. A woman may disappear

in a grocery store where there are no windows,
only aisles of food trapped in boxes or jars.
She may vanish in a magic act like a rabbit

or a handkerchief. Pretty women disappear
as they grow older: suddenly unseen
in the street. A woman can disappear

into the world's expectations: small shoes,
small houses. She may find herself visible
to the people she hopes to please but invisible

to herself. Sometimes a woman disappears
in plain sight: as if wrapped in fog. Amelia Earhart
vanished when she was just my age;

Is she still flying around the world?
Sacagewea disappeared after helping
Lewis and Clark: two languages inside her.

Did she die or find a tribe? There have been
years when my desires were as hidden
as foxes, years when I spoke to my mirror

hoping it would know my chances. I have
disappeared because I was afraid:
as helpless as a chameleon on a leaf.

(stanza break)

Dusting, women have erased themselves
from whole eras of history; each corset
we tightened made us smaller.

Dust

It clings to all our possessions,
fills the distant holes of space. Dust goes
where the wind suggests and it is related
to everything: collapsing stars, seeds,
skin, pollen, bone, feather, blood.

Out of dust things are made; into dust
they disappear. Dust is one reason
we see light; it surrounds planets,
circles galaxies, hides in the closets
of philosophers. Before microscopes,

dust was the smallest thing
we could perceive. Even stones
and elephant tusks add themselves,
little by little, to dust. It floats over
the clutter of home and the honking

of cities, over mountains and murders.
Volcanoes form dust clouds that rise
to the edge of the atmosphere.
Every business makes
its own dust so the dust of war

is different from the dust of peace,
and the dust of hospitals is different
from the dust of newspapers. It has been
called beggar's velvet or house moss;
it was once the edge of the world,

the place where what could be seen
gave way to magic or imagination.
It is what we come from and what
we will return to, what Peter Pan used to fly,
what gathers under the stillness of our beds.

Mountain Lion

for Jerald Murdock

It was not yet spring, just before your father died,
when I saw the mountain lion. Twilight,
when the world prepares
to vanish, and I was driving the steady incline
to our cabin. We were used to the deer which appear
and disappear into their long-legged silences,
their white tails made of escapes; I had seen
owls turning their heads until the past
and present were joined. For weeks the starlings
arranged themselves into elegant temporary patterns
as unpredictable as happiness. This was my first
lion outside a zoo so I was unprepared for
his size and the color of his fur which reminded me
of sunlight burning fields of wheat. Your farher
was sleeping between worlds when I saw him
turning, his power around him like a robe:
a lion disappearing into our forest.

Finding the Dog

Inside the house, where the dog was an idea,
I had no opinion and I did not look. I dreamed
her drowning in the mouth of the bay
but it was my mother who floated
in a canoe with a rope to pull her home
and my sister who carried her to shore.
This was the dog who stood beside
my father after his surgeries,
the one who waited for him in the afternoons,
her fur the color of devotion.
Where was my father? In a courtroom,
making an argument. He knew she was
missing but still hoped she was
not gone. I dreamed the way
she went into the sea: seeking relief
from seizures, the August heat.
Even now, that afternoon
is unbreathable. It was my mother
and sister who struggled with her
remains as she lay heavily
between them; my mother wanted
her buried in the yard where she
had stood, so many afternoons,
beneath a thin pine tree. But my sister
said wild animals would dig her up,
our hole would never work;
she wanted her cremated, on the mantle,
where she could not be taken twice.
Inside the house, where the dog
was an idea, I had no opinion
and I did not look. It was my job
to see things but not touch them,
to watch but offer no advice.
It was my job to know where
the dog could be found but not
to find the dog; not then.

Band Shoes

Now I am past forty I cannot see clearly and reading
each small or distant word has become an act
of imagination. If I make out a few letters my mind
supplies the others, quickly, based on context.
This is an imperfect process in which pets have become

pests and children have turned into chihuahuas;
I have found wonder when I should have found winter,
birds instead of bills. Likewise, my hearing,
never reliable, brings me incomplete sentences,
distorted words, sounds I supply with meaning.

I answer the wrong questions at a dinner party:
tell the man who asks where I'm traveling next
about a number of interesting texts; the lady
who compliments my hat is given my complete history
with cats. It is embarrassing but also pleasant

to live in a place where I write the signs and ask
the questions. In my haze, hotels allow circus animals
instead of service animals and I am happier imagining
an elephant in the elevator, a lion ordering room service.
I answer the question I wish someone would ask,
turn bad news into band shoes.

Typhoid Mary

She meant to give up cooking but she needed the money
and she didn't believe she carried anything deadly;
she changed her name and went from
one wealthy household to another: baking fever
into roasts and pies, pouring glasses of warm death
that the children took so gently to bed. She made
cookies that tasted like the witch's house
in Hansel and Gretel's forest, sliced apples
that might have once belonged to Snow White's stepmother.
She was caught, and caught again, then placed
on an island where she could only cook for herself
and a dog who, I imagine, enjoyed the ribs
she roasted slowly, the chicken soup that simmered
all day on the stove. She was a cook who was not allowed
to cook, the carrier of a germ she could not feel or see.
She was alone in the kitchen: eating the details
she poured and sifted and cut. She didn't
mean to kill yet, behind her, a path of destruction:
empty bedrooms where babies once slept,
silent stairs, sickness like sugar on her hands.

Bears

We walked in those mountains for years: before my brother
made himself from the details of late summer,
when my sister was still the size of a cat. My mother hired
a woman to take care of us so she could sit
between the trees and sketch. We stayed
in a cabin without televisions or telephones,
the woods gathered thickly in our windows.
The animals that walked past us on the way
to the dining hall or lodge seemed gentle --
silent, speckled deer on elegant legs, skunks
embarrassed by their white stripes, squirrels
with impatient tails. Then, one year, we opened
the door and found a bear: vast and black,
standing beside our picnic table, searching
for berries. Later, driving to the place where
we rode horses, a bear with one injured paw
crossed in front of our car, slowly, on his way
to some darker region. Then a bear in a tree
when my father was walking his dog, a bear
in the parking lot while my aunts hid in the gift shop.
The rangers were suddenly small in their
beige costumes. This was the same summer
I saw an albino squirrel: dangerously pale
in a land of shadows. The bears had come to claim
what was theirs, or maybe they had been there
all along but we refused to see them.
We were supposed to make noises on the trail,
keep our food off the porch. My father fell
on a hike beside a river. No, my mother broke
her ankle and was carried to a hospital
at the base of the mountain. My sister got
a sunburn, an alarming case of poison ivy.
I spent one fevered night with the stomach flu
while my babysitter held onto my hair.
Sometimes I find my mother's sketches
from that season of accidents: heavy pencil lines

tracing branches and worry, and even these
suggest that the woods were watching us,
waiting impatiently for our losses.

Balloons

Who doesn't love balloons? Brightly colored circles
of happiness, they are attached
to gravity by a string. I have tied them
to my daughter's wrists,
to shopping carts, and kitchen chairs.
Every impulse inside them longs
to leave. They are alive: heads
floating over tails, as restless
as sperm. Some have
freed themselves to stare down
at me, gleefully, from the ceiling. Some have
slipped from my hand
and risen into the evening: so high
I can only imagine
their delight. Holding one I feel
the tug of a fish,
a dog hurrying at the end
of a leash, my own mood
lifting.

Rewind

I like to rewind movies: watch the maid
unfaint and the milk move from the glass
back into the carton. People walk
backwards up staircases,
undress, cup their hands
and a candle's flame reappears. Clocks
unwind, cars retreat, broken objects
reassemble themselves.
I wish I could live my life that way:
sure of the ending, able to unmake
the beds and uncook the dinner.
I would go back to myself before
it all happened, not wise but not
innocent: in my morning mood,
the argument unargued, my face younger.

The Sick Child

after the painting by Edvard Munch

This is the event from which the artist never recovered:
his sister, Sophie, age fifteen, unable to breathe,
propped against a white pillow in a room
of black and green strokes. Sophie is seen
in profile, looking away from us, her face
delicate and luminous, her red hair
made of light. The bottle on the bedside table
has done no good and the woman in the corner
already wears a mourner's black, her face
buried in loss. We know Sophie will never
get better and the blanket over her body
seems as heavy as earth. This is the image
the artist returned to throughout his life.
He searched the details of the scene for
whatever they might reveal, put his sister
back in the last place he could touch her
or speak with her, brought her out
of death's curtains to comfort the living.

My Tribe

When I went to school in New York,
I read the city was so full of people
that somewhere in my immediate vicinity
were nine strangers whose lives

were nearly identical to my own.
They were short women who grew up
in southern towns, their politics
a bit to the left. They liked

Woody Allen's movies and
Bob Dylan's lyrics; they liked Indian food
and secrets and old bookstores
where cats slept on the shelves.

They drank their tea with cream
and spent hours in the bath soaking
away the past. They were trying
to cure their acne with one hundred

little sauces in jars. They had
perfect eyesight, could read in any light,
and preferred a stack of six books
by the bed. They liked

badly funded museums: tilted buildings,
creepy tour guides, curiosities
under glass. I thought of my unseen tribe
when I was riding the subway

and I saw my own stubborn mouth
on the girl across from me; I thought of them
when it rained: how, like me,
they could never get warm again

(stanza break)

once they were wet, how they
could not open or close their umbrellas.
They were crushed by something
a friend said to them but were trying

not to show it. They were behind me
or ahead of me on the street,
peering into the same windows
that attracted my attention.

They were thinking of the parties
they did not want to attend. I felt better
and worse knowing they were out there:
less alone and less special.

When I was sick I imagined them
under quilts, taking too much vitamin C
but refusing cold medicine. If I was sad
I thought of them on the dark stairs

of their own buildings, dragging bags
of wilted groceries into a kitchen
they hated. I wanted to meet one
of them but worried I wouldn't

like them. Maybe I did meet them
but I didn't know? I am a little
self absorbed. At some point
our lives diverged: I left

New York, moved every few years,
had a daughter. Is this
what happened to them too?
I had the sense, leaving the city,

that my tribe grew smaller.
But maybe it changed?
Suddenly I was related to
housewives and part time

(stanza break)

English teachers: people who were
marginal and hidden. My tribe
didn't go out so there wasn't much
chance that I would run into them

though once, at the park, my daughter
in a stroller, I saw a woman
from behind who I thought might be
myself and I followed

her rustling skirt, her laughter,
her undone hair. She smelled like
someone I used to know but refused
to enjoy. I followed her

until I could not see her
anymore, until I was lost
and breathless
and unsure.

The Sound of a Train

Even now, I hear one and I long to leave
without a suitcase or a plan; I want to step
onto the platform and reach for
the porter's hand and buy a ticket
to some other life; I want to sit
in the big seats and watch fields
turn into rivers or cities. I want to eat
cake on the dining car's
unsteady tablecloths, to sleep
while whole seasons
slip by. I want to be a passenger
again: a person who hears the name
of a place and stands up, a person
who steps into the steam of arrival.

The Town Where I Belong

The town where I belong has no cars, no churches, no gossip.
Here it is always midsummer and the light tastes like laughter.
Every restaurant serves iced tea and every house
has a porch and a bathtub with feet. Books are on shelves

in fields near a lake where the water is so warm
it must come from the kingdom of luck. In this town
my feet don't hurt and I don't carry a purse full of burdens.
There are no calendars, dividing the day into boxes,

no clocks pointing their hands at all the things
I have lost. I spend years sitting in a restaurant
in a forest where trees watch over me like Gods.
Old friends pass through just long enough to drink wine

and sit on a branch made of memory,
then they return to the dust of my dreams. The dead
rent rooms in a hotel above a saloon
and sometimes my favorite writers are up there

with typewriters and cigarettes. There are no holidays,
no taxes, no hospitals. There is no housework;
there are no dull errands or appointments. All the houses
stand open and they smell like wind and ocean,

like freedom. My daughter is happy and tall
and her favorite spiders are spinning webs around the lake
where we swim. This town has no name and no highway
runs through it. My husband is a kind stranger

who takes me on picnics where there are no bees
or thunderstorms. My town has no disappointment,
no money or failure. When I walk through
the old dirt streets or through the shadows

(stanza break)

of the forest I see my mother in a cottage painting
and listening to Italian opera; I find my father beside
the dog he loved best: the one with fur the color of autumn.
There is a fireplace where the answers to all the impossible
questions are as eager and soothing as flames.

Girl on a Swing

She is my mother, perhaps, strung between two worlds;
she is my daughter on a summer playground
with her hands on twin ropes. Even now my grandmother

is pushing me through the lyrics of a song
about a chariot that is sweet and low. In paintings
the girl on a swing is so often turned away from us

and her back suggests that she is about to open
a door made of sky. She longs to leave
yet she longs to return; she asks to go higher.

CPSIA information can be obtained
at www.ICGtesting.com
Printed in the USA
FSOW01n0647240315
5944FS